I0059425

From Successful Business to Personal Financial Security

A Wealth Management

Road Map for Entrepreneurs

and Their Families

Derek M. Mohamed, CRPC ®, AAMS®

Table of Contents

To the memory of my late father, who forever

will be my role model and mentor. He was hard-working,

loving and smart. Sadly, he passed away long before he had the

opportunity to see how much I learned from his example and the

success I have achieved as a result. And to my mother,

whose strength and ever-lasting optimism

has always been an inspiration to me.

To my wife and best friend Nicole, for all of her

love, support and encouragement over the years, and to our

children David, Bella and Zachary, for the joy they bring into

my life and making me smile every day.

Acknowledgements

I WOULD LIKE TO EXPRESS MY GRATITUDE TO THE many wonderfuL people who helped bring my book to completion. Specifically, to those individuals who provided coaching, support, education and who assisted in the writing, editing, proofreading and design, thank you so much. In particular, I would like to thank my friends at CEG Worldwide, including John Bowen, CEO; Allyson Lee, Elite Advisor Coach; Jonathan Powell, Managing Principal; Dianna Orgain, Senior Project Manager; and Katie Soden, Senior Editor. I learned a lot from all of you, which made the book an enjoyable endeavor. Thanks to industry writer and editor, Sydney LeBlanc, for her help in navigating us through the book writing process.

To my team members—Jonathan Penta, Justin Merola, Shawn Devaney, Stephen Greene, Sandy Capobianco and Ellen Barry— thank you all for your partnership and friendship, and for your commitment to helping serve our clients well. Thanks to my expert team members—Bill Shad, Wealth Management Consultant, UBS Wealth Management; Andrew Vanderslice, Risk Management Consultant, UBS Wealth Management; Mike Stowe, Partner, Stowe & Degon LLC; David Degon, Partner,

Stowe & Degon, LLC; Paul Gilligan, Tax Partner; Robert Arone, Partner, Trust and Estate Attorney, Orsi Arone Rothenberg; and Jeff Bell, Estate Planning Specialist, Northeast Brokerage—whose commitment to collaboration is instrumental in achieving wealth management success and is a key point in the book.

Our UBS leadership, including Richard Lown, Managing Director, Complex Director, UBS; Steve Brown, Managing Director, Complex Director, UBS; David McWilliams, Head, Wealth Management Transformation, UBS; and Paul Santucci, COO, UBS Wealth Management Advisor Group, supported our efforts to educate investors through the pages of this book. Thank you.

Special thanks go to our clients who throughout the process of writing this book remained advocates for the advisor-client relationship and proponents of investor education. We appreciate your business, your friendship and your continued trust and confidence.

Last, but not least: I must apologize to those who have helped and inspired me throughout this process and whose names I have failed to mention. Strategic alliances, friends, colleagues and others whose words of inspiration meant so much to me and my team, I thank you.

Introduction

FOR MANY BUSINESS OWNERS AND ENTREPRENEURS, this is both a challenging and exciting time in the financial world. You are facing difficult choices and asking serious questions about achieving your financial goals. It is my hope that the information contained in this book will help you navigate through the noise of the marketplace and make informed decisions about your money.

As a successful entrepreneur, you think and act differently from the rest. You possess ambition fueled by the desire to create unique solutions, quench unmet needs in the market place and solve the long-standing problems for the ever-fickle consumer. From conception to exit, you embrace the critical, yet seldom adhered-to reality that inspiration without perspiration is meaningless. You sacrifice time and resources to the utmost extent and assume the identity, purpose and spirit of the enterprise. In order to be successful as an entrepreneur you need to have a unique and unrivaled focus. You plan each step toward the ultimate success of your venture. The goal is to "win" and you are undeniably committed.

Previously a black hole in many entrepreneurs' lives, wealth management when done properly is a proactive means of helping you achieve peace of mind and financial stability, for yourself and your family, before and after your exit from the business. And when wealth management is practiced effectively, it is a collaborative, customized and comprehensive planning process.

Many entrepreneurs are confused not only about investing, but also about other important financial decisions. In fact, if you're not at least a little confused, you may not be paying attention to what's going on out there. Remember, your financial concerns and the decisions you make can affect your future either in a negative or a positive way. A wealth management approach to financial planning bridges the gap between the entrepreneur and personal finance and helps preserve the entrepreneur's "win" in a liquidity event.

Now, let me ask you this: Have you reflected lately on what's important to you about money? Take a few minutes to really think about the first thing that comes to your mind. Is it having peace of mind? Taking care of your family?

I ask you this question because money means different things to different people. When asking yourself what's important to you about money, you may think of a number of different things. For example, financial independence may be the first thing you think of. Or it could be to take excellent care of your family, to buy whatever you want or need, or maybe it's something as simple as just not having to constantly worry about it.

In this book, we want to help you achieve peace of mind by specifically addressing the unique issues you face with your personal financial situation as a result of being an entrepreneur, not necessarily your business concerns. You already have professionals and a process in place to help you make decisions about your business. However, many of you do not have as efficient a process in place to help you make smart decisions about your personal life with regard to the narratives that arise as a result of being an entrepreneur.

For the purposes of this book, we will cover issues for those entrepreneurs who have had, or expect to have, a life-changing liquidity event. We will also focus on the process of integrated wealth management that helps simplify the decision-making process for you which can result in better personal financial decisions.

We want to help you accomplish these goals and to help you to make informed decisions about your money. In addition to being the CEO in your professional life, you are also the CEO of your family, which is a big responsibility. I believe my book will be a good start in helping you achieve all of these objectives.

Chapter 1

Live the Life You Want

"Good fortune is what happens when opportunity meets with planning."

—Thomas A. Edison

I BEGAN THIS CHAPTER WITH ONE OF MY FAVORITE quotes by Edison because I truly believe that planning is a major component of "good fortune." In order to live the lives we want, we need financial independence and peace of mind. And, for this to occur, we need planning and a framework for financial success.

This can be accomplished, but first we have to recognize that, as entrepreneurs, we all have busy lives. We are juggling priorities, whether it's running the day-to-day operations of our businesses, pursuing strategic initiatives, or dealing with personnel issues or decisions. The bottom line is that it's hard to stay on top of everything with all of these demands.

That being said, each of us still has that big responsibility that I mentioned earlier—being the Chief Executive Officer of our families. As the CEO, we want to take care of those people who are most important to us. And in order to be successful CEOs of our families we must do these two things:

1. We need to have a solid understanding of where we are now (our current position), where we want to go (our goal), and what there are gaps.

2. We need to determine how we are going to address those gaps.

In order to bridge the gaps, we must have clear-cut strategies and tactics.

Through the pages of this book, you will discover a process that will enable you to cut through all of the confusion in the marketplace and rise above the noise that can distract you. It will help you simplify your financial life so you can consistently make informed decisions about your money, day in and day out. I'll describe the framework that will help you do that.

Wealth Management for Entrepreneurs: The Framework, The Process

Comprehensive wealth management is a step-by-step process that coordinates all of the moving parts of your financial life to help you maximize the probability of achieving all that's important to you— your biggest goals.

This process will enable you to do three things:

1. Systematically address each of your financial concerns

2. Streamline your financial life

3. Help ensure that you are consistently making the smartest possible decisions every day about your money.

Before we go any further, though, let me tell you why I feel so passionately about this process.

My Story

I was blessed to have been born into a fantastic family. I am the son, and an only child, of a father who is second generation here in the U.S. and a mother who is first generation. There was no college education in my family on either side, and certainly no family wealth, but through good old-fashioned hard work, my parents were able to provide a comfortable middle-class life for our small family as I was growing up.

I knew that we weren't wealthy by any means, but I never worried about money. In fact, I never really thought about it at all through most of my youth. Fast-forward to November 22, 1994. I was home from college on Thanksgiving break and was heading back to my family's home after a night out with some friends. I was about a mile from home, when an ambulance driving at a high rate of speed passed me in the opposite direction with lights on and siren blazing. Time slowed down, and then it stopped … right then and there. I don't know why, but I just knew something wasn't right.

When I got to my home, all of the lights were on, which was very unusual because it was late in the evening. The doors were open and my parents weren't there. Now, there were no cell phones back then so I couldn't just pick up the phone and call my parents. Instead, I called the police department and they confirmed that an ambulance had been sent to my house and had gone to the hospital. As I got back into my car, I prepared myself for the worst and drove to the hospital. Later that night, my father passed away after having had a massive heart attack. I was 19 years old. Very suddenly, my life changed dramatically. Obviously, losing a parent is a major event for anyone, but the life I had led where I never had to worry about money, that also changed.

While we weren't destitute, my family had not done any financial planning. My father had a very small life insurance policy and a small retirement account, but that was about it. Unfortunately, over the next several years, I had to watch my mother work a lot harder than she should have. I also worked several jobs to pay for college and lived at home instead of on campus. We were able to scratch and claw to get by, but things were a lot more difficult than they should have been.

When I began my career, I realized that there were many other families who could be in a similar situation without our help. While the families we work with today are quite a bit wealthier than my family was, I see a lot of commonalities.

Unfortunately, there are so many successful entrepreneurs who are so very busy with their daily lives and running businesses that they let their personal financial matters fall to the bottom of the priority list. With a little guidance, we can help put them and their families in a position to have much better outcomes.

That's why I'm so passionate about this doing this.

Major Areas of Financial Concern

When I talk to successful entrepreneurs about their liquidity events, time and again, my team and I at UBS find that there are five major areas of financial concern. They are:

First—Preserving your wealth in order to fund all of your goals.

Second—Mitigating and minimizing your income taxes and maximizing your cash flow.

Third—Taking care of your heirs and making sure your assets are distributed efficiently.

Fourth—Protecting your assets so that they're not wrongly taken and you're not exposed to unnecessary risks that could negatively impact your family.

Fifth—Exploring charitable giving. We find that a number of our clients are very charitably minded and want to make sure their charitable gifts are impactful.

To effectively address each of these five challenges, we believe you need comprehensive wealth management. You should start with these three things:

1. Use a consultative process to gain a detailed understanding of your deepest values and goals as well as your most important needs and wants.

2. Develop customized solutions that are designed to fit your unique situation beyond simply investments. Unfortunately, most individuals and financial advisors tend to focus only on the investments. They don't deal with the other pressing financial challenges we all face.

3. Implement the solutions in close consultation with your other professional advisors as a team. Some families act in isolation without coordination among the various experts such as accountants, attorneys, life insurance specialists and other professionals. It's much more efficient to make these decisions and implement the strategies in collaboration with your team of professional advisors.

Chapter 2

Wealth Management Today: The Three Pillars

WHILE THE ENTREPRENEUR METICULOUSLY PLANS for the success of the enterprise, personal finance seldom, if ever, garners the attention it deserves. The transition from wealth creation to wealth management is a critical stage in the life cycle of the entrepreneur. Immediately pre- or post-liquidity event, successful entrepreneurs may find themselves besieged by decisions and variables over which they have little control. Accustomed to complete and final control, this uncertainty may lead the entrepreneur to avoid key decisions which can create the potential for personal financial turmoil. Despite earning some of the biggest paydays, successful entrepreneurs must take care to ensure that the big win is not lost. Unfortunately, in the time frame leading up to and immediately following a major liquidity event, wealth management and its processes are often poorly defined in the mind of the entrepreneur.

Let me share with you how our team thinks about wealth management. Wealth management, frankly, is one of the most overused and misused terms in finance today. If you ask five different investors what wealth management means I'm sure you'll get five different answers. Not surprisingly, if you ask five wealth managers what wealth management is, I think you'll also get five different answers. Wealth management really contains three components (or pillars)—Investment Consulting, Advanced Planning and Relationship Management.

Redefining Wealth Management

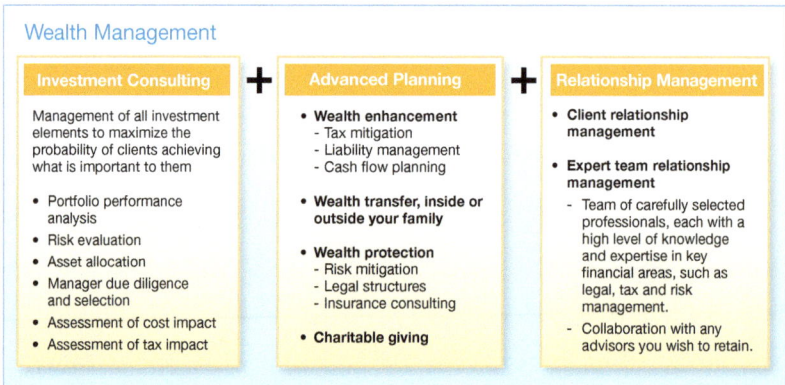

Wealth Management		
Investment Consulting	**Advanced Planning**	**Relationship Management**
Management of all investment elements to maximize the probability of clients achieving what is important to them	• **Wealth enhancement** - Tax mitigation - Liability management - Cash flow planning	• **Client relationship management**
• Portfolio performance analysis	• **Wealth transfer, inside or outside your family**	• **Expert team relationship management** - Team of carefully selected professionals, each with a high level of knowledge and expertise in key financial areas, such as legal, tax and risk management.
• Risk evaluation	• **Wealth protection**	
• Asset allocation	- Risk mitigation	
• Manager due diligence and selection	- Legal structures - Insurance consulting	
• Assessment of cost impact	• **Charitable giving**	- Collaboration with any advisors you wish to retain.
• Assessment of tax impact		

The first pillar is "investment consulting" and focuses on managing capital. Volumes have been written about how to invest successfully and there is no shortage of advisors willing to help you with this aspect of wealth management. Some do it better than others, of course.

The second pillar is "advanced planning" and it consists of four components: wealth enhancement, wealth transfer, wealth protection and charitable giving. I'll discuss those components in detail later in the chapter.

The third pillar of wealth management is "relationship management," which has two aspects. First, client relationship management and second, expert team relationship management. This involves managing the wealth management process itself, as well as managing and integrating the professionals who will coordinate and collaborate to bring the best solutions for families and individuals.

Investment Consulting: The First Pillar

Let's start with the first pillar, investment consulting, and its definition and process. Then we'll move on to the four advanced planning areas.

I believe there are six critical investment consulting steps to preserve and grow your wealth. They are:

First—Create a lifetime cash flow needs analysis. This is a cash flow model that quantifies exactly what is going to be needed to fund your goals over the rest of your lifetime. It takes into account assumptions about portfolio rate of return, inflation and other factors, and provides stress and probabilistic scenario testing.

Second—Determine a target rate of return for your investment portfolio. This needs to be done in conjunction with the cash flow needs analysis, and the target rate of return should be the rate of return that makes everything work to your satisfaction in the cash flow needs analysis.

Third—Design an optimized asset allocation strategy for your target rate of return. Once you know what that target rate of return is, you want to have an asset allocation strategy that is designed to achieve that target rate of return with the least amount of risk and volatility as possible. Of course, make sure that this allocation is going to be appropriate for your level of risk tolerance.

Fourth—Decide which investment vehicles you'll use. Are you going to pick the stocks and bonds? Are you going to use mutual funds or institutional money managers, or will you use exchange-traded funds (ETFs)? Which other investment vehicles will you use? Will you use any alternative investments?

Fifth—Document your investment strategy; put it in writing.

Sixth—Track your investment progress on a regular basis. This should be in writing as well. Are you going to track it quarterly, semi-annually, annually? I would advise against doing it daily, however.

Advanced Planning: The Second Pillar

Wealth Enhancement

If you're like most successful families and other successful entrepreneurs, you're concerned with more than just investments. I already mentioned the four advanced planning concerns which are wealth enhancement, wealth transfer, wealth protection and charitable giving. So, let's start with the first concern, wealth enhancement: mitigating or minimizing income and taxes, and maximizing cash flow. Let me share with you the top ten strategies we see successful families deploying. (See chart below.)

Top Strategies for Wealth Enhancement

1. Review last two years of tax returns to determine a baseline
2. Perform a current year tax assessment
3. Evaluate benefits plan
4. Analyze executive compensation program
5. Assess retirement plan structure
6. Assess education funding plan
7. Assess existing credit facilities
8. Consider business structure(s) and alternate options
9. Conduct scenario modeling for special planning opportunities
10. Establish SMART priorities

You should start with a review of recent tax returns to determine a baseline, then perform a current year tax assessment. Your benefits plan should then be evaluated. Next, you will want to analyze your executive compensation program that is in place and assess the retirement plan structure. At this point, your education funding plan for your children or for your grandchildren should be assessed as well. The same should be done for your existing credit facilities and evaluate the liability side of your balance sheet.

Let's consider different business structures now. You need to analyze how everything is titled and structured currently, and then review alternate business structures and options. Scenario modeling is an important next step. We call this modeling "what-if planning" in order to look at special planning opportunities. The last step (and you'll see this throughout the various sections) is to establish SMART priorities. It's an acronym you're probably familiar with, but in establishing any goals or objectives, you want those objectives to be Specific, Measurable, Achievable, Realistic and Time bound. We want them to be SMART.

Have you established your own SMART goals?
- Specific
- Measurable
- Achievable
- Realistic
- Time bound

Advanced Planning: Wealth Transfer

Next, let's consider the top ten strategies we see successful families using to take care of their heirs. Please see the chart below:

Top Strategies for Wealth Transfer

1. Identify wealth-transfer preferences
2. Review existing estate planning documents
3. Identify any special situations
4. Confirm correct titling of assets
5. Confirm proper funding of trusts
6. Ensure correct designation of beneficiaries
7. Document wishes regarding end-of-life issues
8. Provide for business succession
9. Provide for liquidity needs
10. Establish SMART priorities

First, identify your wealth transfer preferences. Ask yourself these questions: Where do you want the money to go? Are there special circumstances within your family? Do you have any children who might be particularly successful or who may need financial assistance? Do you have a child (or children) who has special needs considerations? It's smart to start by identifying the preferences that you have up front. It's a place you need to start.

Next, it's time to review the existing estate planning documents that you have in place, and to identify any special situations, such as a family dynamic. You want to confirm that you have correct titling of your assets. If you have estate planning documents in place, you will want to confirm that you funded the trusts that were intended to be funded, and made any titling changes that were intended to have been made.

Oftentimes, we see families with a thick binder of estate planning documents that established a well- thought-out plan that was never implemented, or with items that fell through the cracks, such as ensuring that the correct designation of beneficiaries are assigned, particularly on retirement accounts and insurance policies.

You also need to document your wishes regarding end of life issues. Do you want heroic measures to be taken if you're incapacitated? There are many other details around those considerations that need to be discussed.

There are numerous issues that can arise with business succession, regardless of whether there are family members in the business or not. How are you going to transition the leadership of the business you've worked so hard to build? You need to provide for liquidity needs. A big concern of many entrepreneurs who are putting all of their capital into the business, particularly in the start-up phase, is how to create liquidity outside the business. Again, you'll see the recurring theme of establishing some SMART priorities.

Advanced Planning: Wealth Protection

Wealth protection is about protecting ourselves and our loved ones, protecting our confidential information, our financial assets and our property from being wrongly or improperly taken. This is the third advanced planning concern. We see successful entrepreneurs and their families using the ten strategies listed in the chart below in each of these areas.

Top Strategies for Wealth Protection

1. Brainstorm about and quantify exposures to risks
2. Leverage asset-protection strategies
3. Get second opinions on all major financial transactions
4. Verify that your life insurance is adequate
5. Evaluate your property-casualty insurance
6. Consider umbrella liability coverage
7. Verify that your health and disability coverage is adequate
8. Consider long-term care insurance
9. Evaluate your commercial insurance coverage
10. Establish SMART priorities

First, brainstorm with your family members and/or with your other professional advisors about the different risks you have, what exposures you have, and then quantify them. Next, it's important to leverage asset protection strategies, which could be legal structures and titling of assets for asset protection. Then you want to always get a second opinion on major financial transactions to make sure you are not overlooking any risks.

After that, you need to confirm that your life insurance is adequate, evaluate your property-casualty insurance and consider umbrella liability coverage. Also verify that your health and disability coverage is adequate. You will want to consider long-term care insurance and evaluate your commercial insurance coverage. Finally, of course, establish your SMART priorities.

Advanced Planning: Charitable Giving

Let's now move on to the fourth advanced planning concern: charitable giving. To the extent that successful entrepreneurs and their families want to make their charitable gifts even more impactful, they must deal effectively with the numerous issues surrounding gifting.

Top Strategies for Charitable Giving

1. Determine your charitable intent
2. Consider checkbook philanthropy or volunteering
3. Consider will bequest
4. Consider community foundations or private foundations
5. Consider donor-advised funds
6. Consider life insurance
7. Consider charitable gift annuities
8. Consider charitable remainder or charitable lead trusts
9. Consider lead trusts
10. Establish SMART priorities

Each of the ten actions listed above have many nuances. The first step is to determine your charitable intent. The most basic way to make a charitable difference, of course, is through volunteering time, and/or making small, direct donations.

However, in some cases, more sophisticated strategies should be considered in conjunction. Perhaps you should think about a bequest. Consider community foundations, private foundations, donor-advised funds, and life insurance in a charitable context. Additional strategies include charitable gift annuities, charitable remainder trusts, or charitable lead trusts. You'll need to educate yourself about these strategies, or find someone to help you. Next, of course, you need to establish your SMART priorities.

In order to address each of the five major financial concerns that our clients at UBS typically have—preserving wealth, mitigating taxes, taking care of heirs, making sure that assets are not wrongly taken and charitable giving—we use a distinctive process. Whether you manage your own finances or you're working with a wealth manager who assists you as your family's CFO, the following is the process we recommend you use:

Our Five-Step Consultative Process

Discovery meeting	Wealth management plan meeting	Mutual commitment meeting	Advanced planning meeting	Regular progress meetings
Complete discovery process	High-level presentation of wealth management solutions	Confirmation of commitment	Prioritize and set timelines for implementing wealth management strategies	Review of progress and implementation of advanced plan

Financial goal analysis and investment strategy review
Financial planning diagnostic of current situation and strategic recommendations for moving forward

The advanced plan
Comprehensive evaluation of the entire range of financial needs with our recommendations for moving forward

The expert team
Team of carefully selected professionals, each with a high level of knowledge and expertise in key financial areas

Expert team meeting
Together with our team of specialists, we apply our expertise to evaluate all aspects of your financial situation and devise appropriate solutions.

First Step: Discovery Meeting

First, it's important to start with a "discovery meeting" and this is something you can do on your own or with the help of a wealth manager. The idea is to first develop a total family profile to look at where you are now and where you want to go. That total family profile should be divided into seven sections: values, relationships, goals, financial information and assets, advisors, process and interests.

- First, you need to clearly understand your values. What's important about money to you personally? What are your three biggest financial concerns?

- What are the most important relationships you have? They can be your parents, siblings, children, friends or people in the community who are very important to you. One of your most important relationships may even be an organization or an entity to which you have strong ties, such as a religious organization or church.

- Next, you want to think about your goals. Where do you want to be in ten years, in 15 years? What would you like to achieve going forward?

- Then, you want to look at your financial situation and take an inventory of your assets and your liabilities.

- Now, list your professional advisors who have a seat at your table in helping you make smart decisions. Who are your professional advisors?

- Given all the distractions that we discussed earlier, research shows that a vast majority of investors don't have a process for reaching their goals, and surprisingly, they don't believe that their financial advisor has an organized process to solve all of their challenges. So, what's the process you're going to use to make sure you stay on track for achieving your goals?

- And something else that is essential to your total family profile—as an entrepreneur, what do you want to do when you are not working? What do you enjoy doing and what are your interests?

After you construct your total family profile, you'll want to do the lifetime cash flow analysis discussed earlier. At this point, you will have a clear understanding of where you are now, where you want to go, and the gaps that exist.

Second Step: Wealth Management Plan Meeting

Now you need to develop an investment strategy and solutions to your other wealth management issues. (If you're doing this on your own, remember to put it in writing.) During the wealth management meeting or meetings, overall key concerns from a wealth management perspective are discussed and the investment plan is drafted.

After the meeting (if you are working with a competent and skilled wealth manager), and once the investment plan is drafted, we advise our own clients to take it home, digest it and bring it back to the next meeting with any questions. If you're doing your own wealth management planning, ideally, put the plan aside for a week, then review it to make sure it accurately reflects where you are now and where you want to go, and that it's aligned with your risk/return profile.

Third Step: Mutual Commitment Meeting

We have a mutual commitment meeting with our clients as part of our five-step process. In this step, we look at the draft of the investment plan, the key concerns of the wealth management issues, and then we do any necessary fine-tuning. Of course, there may be issues that are unresolved on either side, so this is the time to ask any questions, and where we typically ask questions and express any concerns about moving forward as well. We may decide that we are not a 100 percent good fit for each other. Then both parties make a decision, and if it is a good fit, then the working agreement is formalized.

Now it's time to put the plan in to place.

To do this, your expert team of accountants, attorneys and other professionals should meet to review your total family profile. Their job is to brainstorm about actions that you should take to address the four advanced planning concerns (wealth enhancement, wealth transfer, wealth protection and charitable giving) and then prioritize these actions for your review. We do this in a formal expert team meeting held on a monthly basis on behalf of our clients. This is something you should do if you don't have a wealth manager handling it for you.

Fourth Step: Advanced Planning Meeting

In this meeting, you need to prioritize and set timelines for implementing the SMART priorities in each of the advanced planning areas. As we mentioned earlier, there is a SMART priority decision-making process for wealth transfer, wealth protection, wealth enhancement and charitable giving. You need to prioritize these now during the advanced planning meeting.

Fifth Step: Regular Progress Meetings

Once you've completed the process, it's important to schedule regular progress meetings. Schedule them for yourself or schedule them with your wealth manager at a frequency that makes sense for your situation, whether it's monthly, quarterly or semi-annually—but at the absolute minimum, annually. Either way, be sure you're having regular progress meetings. Every time you do this, you should review these three things:

- Has anything changed personally, professionally or financially?

- Are you on track with your investments, and is there any fine-tuning that needs to be done?

- What advanced planning strategies and tactics are in process right now? What's the status? Are there any new strategies or tactics that should be implemented now?

Remember, whether you're working with a wealth manager to facilitate this for you, or you choose to do it on your own, you are your family's CEO. You might be co-CEO with your spouse but you're still CEO of your own family. Whether you have a large family or you're single, whether you are an entrepreneur who owns a large business or you're simply earning a paycheck, you are responsible for making all of these major decisions.

Relationship Management: The Third Pillar

Now, as CEO, you're going to need to some help. There's no one person who's an expert in all areas, so we have been stressing the importance of building a team. As entrepreneurs, this is intuitive. You know this in your professional life and it's the same for your personal financial life. As you build your team, you need to get all team members working collaboratively. We have found that for most successful families, the core expert team consists of a wealth manager who acts as the personal CFO and facilitates the process. To remind you, at a minimum it also consists of an accountant, a private client lawyer or trusts and estate specialist, and an insurance specialist. Other experts can be brought in on an as-needed basis. The wealth manager is able to leverage his or her relationship with the expert team to develop a comprehensive plan.

Chapter 3

What You've Learned as Your Family's CEO

LET'S REVIEW WHAT WE'VE OUTLINED SO FAR IN THE book. First, if you are acting as both your family's CEO and CFO, I suggested you need to develop your total family profile. You need a clear understanding of where you are now, where you want to go and what the gaps are. Next, you have to formulate an investment strategy or an investment plan. You'll want to use the six steps we discussed so you don't make any costly mistakes.

Again, those steps are:

First—Create a lifetime cash flow needs analysis.

Second—Determine a target rate of return.

Third—Design an optimized asset allocation strategy that's going to have a high probably of driving the returns you need with an appropriate amount of risks.

Fourth—Decide on the actual investment vehicles you're going to use.

Fifth—Put it in writing; document your strategy.

Sixth—Track your progress regularly.

Also, you'll also need to develop an advanced plan so that you're not only preserving your wealth and growing it, but you're also mitigating income tax through wealth enhancement. You're also taking care of your heirs through wealth transfer and using wealth protection to ensure your assets are not unjustly taken from you. Next, you should address your charitable giving concerns. Most likely, you will need some help in each of these areas—so who do you have helping you? Right!—Your expert team.

If you're acting as both your family's CEO and the CFO, you also need to ask yourself: Are you doing it right? We find that more than four out of five successful entrepreneurs and families today are second-guessing whether or not they're doing it right. As we mentioned several times throughout the book, one of your biggest challenges as your family's CEO is to thoughtfully evaluate where you are now and identify the gaps between that and where you're trying to go. The wealth management consultative process has been the most efficient means of addressing these issues successfully with the families and entrepreneurs we work with.

Chapter 4

Be Successful on Purpose

I BELIEVE I HAVE OUTLINED AND EXPLAINED the most effective framework for overseeing your finances: comprehensive wealth management. I shared with you the four advanced planning concerns and other issues and how you might best explore addressing them. Now, it's all up to you. It's an exciting and challenging time to be an entrepreneur and to be the CEO of your family. There are many things going on in the world that, over the next few years, are going to make it extremely rewarding if you design your wealth management plan to be successful.

I want you to be successful on purpose. As an entrepreneur, you owe it to your family, yourself, and your business to make sure that your wealth management plan is well-designed, not only to deal with all the challenges but, more importantly, to take advantage of all the opportunities and maximize the probability of achieving all that's important to you. Planning for your family's financial security is also an essential part of your journey toward your exit, and/or in the years following. A competent wealth manager can steward you through the entire process and help ensure that you keep winning after the "win."

When I started this project, I believed this book would be worthwhile if I could show entrepreneurs how to make smart and informed decisions about their money so they can maximize the probability of achieving all that's important to them and their families. Hopefully, we have been successful in doing that and you have learned a few things about how to make informed decisions about your money.

Chapter 5

Situations, Solutions and Outcomes

I BELIEVE THE BEST WAY FOR US TO ILLUSTRATE HOW we use our wealth management road map in our work with entrepreneurs is to share with you a few case studies. In the case studies below, we have chronicled a unique business/professional situation, as well as the solutions crafted and executed by the team of experts both from within and outside of UBS, and the successful outcome for three entrepreneurs with distinct challenges.

The case studies highlight the team collaboration and the strategies that used to develop integrated and comprehensive wealth management plans for optimal success. We believe that the case studies presented will give you a closer look at how our collaborative and holistic approach to wealth management can help ensure success for your family.

Please note that these case studies are hypothetical and intended only as an illustration of how utilizing the strategies I've outlined and a collaborative approach can help business owners achieve their goals. Please consult your Financial Advisor regarding your specific circumstances.

Case Study: A Surgeon's Silos

Situation:

A successful and well-known surgeon had a thriving practice as well as an ancillary business tied to his practice. Trying to balance the challenges of managing a large practice, his other business, and the demands of being a father to three children, he had decided several years before to hire someone to manage his financial affairs. Choosing to focus his energy on his business activities, he assumed that his financial affairs were being handled by the advisor that he had hired, and that he was in good shape.

In addition to his financial advisor, the doctor had an accountant for his personal affairs, a tax advisor for his practice and his business, a life insurance agent, an insurance agent for his business and practice needs, a business attorney, and an estate planning attorney.

Having been introduced to the team by a mutual friend of his who happened to be an existing physician client, the team provided the doctor a full diagnostic analysis of his situation. As it turned out, despite working for a firm that claimed to be wealth managers, the advisor that the doctor had been working with was really an investment generalist, and there were several wealth management issues that were not addressed.

Solution:

The first step was to aggregate all of the doctor's financial information into one place, and to do a lifetime cash flow needs assessment and scenario diagnostic. With the doctor's permission, the team provided his other advisors online access to the doctor's Financial Goal Analysis and arranged a conference call to discuss it. With each advisor logged in at his or her own office, the team walked through the family's cash flow needs, financial goals, income sources, investment assets, other assets, liabilities, estate planning strategies and insurance coverages. In addition, the team shared several scenarios along with their potential outcomes for the doctor. This was the first time that many of the advisors had ever spoken to one another, and each advisor on the call confessed that he or she learned something new about the doctor's situation. Almost immediately, the advisors began suggesting changes to be made in their respective areas. These suggestions were aggregated and brought back to the doctor for his review.

Outcome:

While describing to the doctor what had happened on this call, he made the observation that he had been managing his finances in silos. Because each advisor in his life was acting independently, by default he was putting the responsibility of facilitating the dialogue between them on his own shoulders, and he realized that he was not doing that effectively. In the end, the doctor decided that he really needed a wealth manager to coordinate his affairs and his other advisors, and not just a single investment advisor. The doctor hired the UBS team to be his family's Chief Financial Officer and financial quarterback. Since then, UBS has helped develop an integrated and comprehensive wealth management plan for his family. The team coordinates an annual call among all of the advisors to ensure that he stays on track.

Case Study: Life Changes

Situation:

An entrepreneur launched her company about ten years ago. After numerous rounds of financing, her business went through a challenging period and she was forced to bootstrap the company. As a result, she was significantly leveraged and went through some very difficult times, missing payments on personal expenditures and teetering on the edge of personal bankruptcy. Thankfully, the economy turned around, the business started to thrive, and became of interest to several competitors in her space.

The client engaged the team to address some planning issues prior to the liquidity event, and the company was acquired in a very large transaction, resulting in a life-changing liquidity event for her. Because of the work that was done up-front, her plan was in place already, and the client was able to implement the strategies efficiently and expeditiously that had been agreed upon. She had an investment strategy that was in line with the return objectives necessary to reach her family's long-term goals, and an expert team of professionals was put in place for her that communicated regularly and openly. She had the financial peace of mind that most entrepreneurs long for.

However, soon after her exit, her life changed. Married for more than 25 years, she and her husband had grown apart and decided to get divorced. Unfortunately, an unforeseen life event had occurred that would force her to re-think all of the wealth planning that had been done previously. There would be a certain impact on her financial situation, and even though the client would still be a multi-millionaire, there was new uncertainty in her life.

Solution:

The UBS team, leveraging a team of outside experts, approached the situation as if working with a brand new client, making no assumptions. This helped the client re-evaluate her long term objectives and priorities, and quantify the changes that would need to be made. The team helped her to prioritize the adjustments and to execute on the implementation of new strategies, as well as navigate the unfortunate logistics of a lengthy and expensive divorce process.

Outcome:

Because the client had her wealth management team in place, and an efficient process for making financial decisions, an unforeseen life event was handled systematically and effectively. The client was extremely thankful that while the plan had to change, the process and people were in place to help her navigate a difficult situation. Now, a few years later, the client once again has the peace of mind she had a few years ago that comes with being financially organized, and is enjoying retirement in Arizona.

Case Study: Getting Your Ducks in a Row

Situation:

An entrepreneur and respected professor started a company with some of his colleagues in which he would have a significant exit within the next three to five years, depending on whether they decided to do a strategic deal or take the company public.

At the initial meeting, he shared the background of his business and approached the UBS team for help in getting his legal affairs in order to transfer some of the ownership of the business to his children for the tax benefits before a deal was eminent.

The initial discussions revealed several other issues that would need to be resolved:

- What are your basic plans after the sale of your business and what will you do with the rest of your life?

- After taxes, how much money do you need to comfortably live the rest of your life?

- How much can you really afford to give away to your children?

- How should gifts be structured to protect your children against creditors or potential future divorce?

- At various exit amount assumptions, what rate of return will you need on your capital to accomplish all of your goals?

- What will happen if you decide you don't want to work again?

Solution:

Utilizing our proprietary wealth management consultative process, the advisor helped the entrepreneur address the issues identified above. The advisor also helped the client to build his own expert team. He had an existing trust and estate attorney with whom he was comfortable, and the advisor introduced him to a tax advisory firm that was better suited to his new situation. Meetings were conducted with the specialists on the expert team and the suggested solutions were brought to the client. The advisor then helped him prioritize the necessary actions in each of the four advanced planning areas: wealth enhancement, wealth transfer, wealth protection and charitable giving.

Outcome:

Because of the upfront work that was done, the client's plan is largely in place already, before the liquidity event has occurred. When it does happen, the advisor and team will be able to implement the strategies efficiently and expeditiously that have been agreed upon. The client has an investment strategy that is in line with the return objectives necessary to reach his long term goals, and he has an expert team of professionals in place that communicates regularly and openly. With all of this in place, he now has the confidence and peace of mind to pursue other interests, and focus on teaching. In addition, he is in the process of starting another venture that he hopes will be even more successful than the first.

Chapter 6

A Second Opinion

MY CALLING IS TO WORK WITH SUCCESSFUL FAMILIES to help them simplify their financial lives and make informed financial decisions acting as their personal CFO. In conjunction with this project, we will make ourselves available to everyone who reads this book, and to anyone who is concerned about whether they're making smart decisions with their money. My team and I will do this by providing you with a second opinion on your finances. We have a robust process with proprietary elements that were perfected through many years of development. We'll take a look at where you are now, where you're trying to go and identify any gaps in order to determine whether you're positioned well with your current provider. If you are, we will recommend that you stay with that individual or team.

If you're not well-positioned, then we'll determine with you if we might be the right firm or the right team to help you achieve all that's important to you. However, we limit our practice to only those families for whom we can have a major impact as their personal CFO. If we're not the right group to help you and you do need to make a change, then we are committed to pointing you in the right direction. We will help you find a competent and experienced professional who should be equipped to serve you well.

If you'd like to receive the complete diagnostic review and our professional opinion of what we would do if we were in your shoes, just send me an email at Derek.Mohamed@ubs.com. Then, I'll have a member of our team call you and schedule an appointment. We'll send a letter confirming the appointment and the information you need to bring with you so that we can make that meeting as productive as possible. If you're interested in our second opinion service and have questions, please also let us know that too. My staff can reach out to you to schedule a phone appointment to discuss your questions. Additional contact information is on the last page of the book.

We wish you nothing but success in achieving all that's important to you. We hope you have enjoyed the book.

Derek Mohamed, CRPC®, AAMS®

Senior Vice President–Wealth Management; Wealth Advisor

The Mohamed-Penta Wealth Management Group

55 William Street, 3rd Floor

Wellesley, MA 02481

781-446-8939 • 800-828-0717

Please visit our website at: http://financialservicesinc.ubs.com/ wealth/E-maildisclaimer.html for important disclosures and information about our e-mail policies. For your protection, please do not transmit orders or instructions by e-mail or include account numbers, Social Security numbers, credit card numbers, passwords, or other personal information.

www.ingramcontent.com/pod-product-compliance
Lightning Source LLC
Chambersburg PA
CBHW041717200326
41520CB00001B/140